I0485862

MoneySmarts:
The Business Of Business
201 SuperEntrepreneur Tips For Instant Business Success!

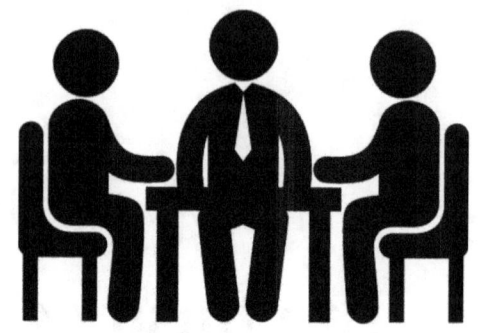

MoneySmarts:
The Business Of Business

Eric Smarts

This book is dedicated to all those who have encouraged & believed in me: family, close friends, business associates, pastors & mentors.

To all the SuperEntrepreneurs who have inspired to me to write this: Gary Vaynerchuck, Jack Dorsey, Marie Forleo, Josh Kaufman, Lewis Howes, Dale Partridge & Matthew Sapaula.

Rodwell, you've been a good friend, teacher and brother and I thank you for your constant positive influence. You're a visionary and an ambassador for divine inspiration & excellence just like me and it's been a privilege knowing you. Thank you.

CONTENTS

TECHNOLOGY

PRODUCT

PITCHING TO INVESTORS

MoneySmarts: The Business Of Business (201 SuperEntrepreneur Tips For Instant Business Success)

Published by Eric Smarts International
London, England NW9 5QG

This publication is designed to provide accurate and authoritative information with regard to the subject matter covered. It is sold with the understanding that the publisher is not engaged in rendering financial, accounting or other professional advice. If financial advice or other expert advice is required, the services of a competent professional should be sought.

Printed in the United Kingdom
ISBN: 978-1517711917

Other Books by Eric Smarts:
MoneySmarts: The Business Edition
MoneySmarts: The Investing Edition
MoneySmarts: The Youth Edition
For The Love Of Money (The Couple's Edition)
The Real M.B.A Model (Marketing, Branding & Advertising)
A Story Of Bible & Business

INTRODUCTION

There are many reasons why people want to start a business. Some want to create a startup for the simple reason of wanting to make money. Others want to live their dream while being financially rewarded. Some decide to go into business because they simply cannot stand working for anyone else (I was the same!) Then there are some who want to accumulate funds as quickly as possible for a specific purpose, such as buying a home, providing an inheritance for their families, or paying for a college education.

To get where you want to go in life, it is important to decide in advance how you will get there. Goals are signposts on the highway to the future. They serve as your guide to personal, career, and financial success. By keeping specific goals in view, you can direct your energies toward achieving your goals.

Every new business owner faces an uphill battle for survival. In fact, financial giant Bloomberg estimates that up to 80 percent of all new small businesses fail within 18 months. Whether you're an entrepreneur running a startup or running a department in a large company, more money must become your mantra. Money is one of those taboo topics in society that we don't like to talk about. We admire athletes and celebrities and envy them for the money they have, yet we get uncomfortable when the "m" word is brought up when it comes to us. Entrepreneurship isn't about selling things - it's about finding innovative ways to improve people's lives. Until recently, most people in business focused on products and services that would appeal to consumers, and this resulted in the creation of many great companies and a lot of jobs. But attitudes are changing. A new generation of entrepreneurs is using approaches from the commercial world and employing technology to tackle social and environmental problems - these areas used to be the exclusive territory of government agencies and charitable organisations. But business is evolving in ways we have never seen. I have these 201 tips for business that will completely revolutionise the way you handle business and enterprise. If there's one thing you can be sure of in life, it's this: You will never know enough. You will always be forced to make a decision without fully understanding what is coming. So be open-minded and ready to learn. As a founder, that is just something you have to get comfortable with. So I have compiled a massive list of rules and laws of business that cover every area of the financial and entrepreneurial stratosphere.

Typically, a "SuperEntrepreneur" is defined as an individual who has founded a new firm and made at least a billion dollars in doing so. Someone self-made, someone who came from nothing and has built an empire in areas such as tech, biotech, finance or retail. I loved this definition prior to writing this book until I realised that not every one who is self-made, successful and driven will amass exactly one billion dollars in revenue. And that's perfectly okay. We are all SuperEntrepreneurs. I believe achievement is key and should be the primary basis of our recognition of others, however, we must never fail to acknowledge the fact before these men and women got to billionaire status, they had been SuperEntrepreneurs way before. My belief is that there is such a thing as the business of business, and together with some famous business quotes from the SuperEntrepreneurial Hall of Fame that come later in the book, there are morsels of information and useful keys that should make this book virtually irreplaceable in your business/financial book collection. Take your time with this, don't try to finish it all in one day. I want to encourage you to absorb and receive these pieces of advice so that you can be the MoneySmart entrepreneur you were created to be. Enjoy!

Eric Smarts, The-Guy-Who-Believes-Everyone-Can-Succeed
Founder & CEO at MoneySmartsSchool.com

Tip #1:

Everyone has great ideas, but not everybody has the ability to follow through. Always find a way to motivate yourself to do what's required to build real success. And remember, it's never going to be about just how hard you work, the secret is in how smart you work.

TIP #2:
TAKE YOUR PERSONAL BRAND SERIOUSLY.
GOOGLE YOURSELF. WHAT SHOWS UP IS YOUR
ONLINE PERSONAL BRAND AND IT'S YOUR JOB TO
MAKE SURE IT IS CLEAN AND ATTRACTIVE TO THE
GENERAL PUBLIC. YOU HAVE SIGNIFICANT
CONTROL OVER HOW YOU ARE PERCEIVED.
NEVER TAKE THIS FOR GRANTED.

Tip #3:

ALWAYS BE THINKING BIG. IF YOU'RE GOING TO BE THINKING ABOUT ANYTHING, YOU MIGHT AS WELL BE THINKING BIG. BIG DREAMS, BIG THOUGHTS, BIG ASPIRATIONS. IF YOU TRULY BELIEVE THAT YOU HAVE AN AMAZING IDEA OR THINK YOU CAN CONVERT IT INTO A PROFITABLE BUSINESS THAT CAN ONE DAY BE EXPANDED AND OPTIMISED FOR GROWTH, THEN GO FOR IT. TIME WASTERS DON'T HAVE TIME TO SUCCEED.

Tip #4:

Do not hesitate when it comes to hiring the best. Hire smart. You're the visionary, so there's no need to enforce authority because they should already know it. Find the best and sell them your story and vision. Never be threatened by people smarter than you. They are the keys to your company's stability, star quality & future success.

TIP #5:

DO WHATEVER IT TAKES TO BUILD SELF-CONFIDENCE AND SELF-ESTEEM AND ATTEND AS MANY BUSINESS NETWORKING EVENTS AS POSSIBLE. EMBRACE EVERY OPPORTUNITY TO SPEAK WITH FELLOW ENTREPRENEURS THAT ARE SMARTER, MORE ESTABLISHED & MORE SUCCESSFUL THAN YOU ARE. IT'S PRICELESS EDUCATION.

TIP #6:
IF YOUR LINKEDIN PROFILE LOOKS LIKE A RESUME OR CV, YOU'VE MISSED THE WHOLE POINT OF LINKEDIN. YOUR PROFILE NEEDS TO LOOK MORE LIKE A SEO LANDING PAGE FOR YOU AND YOUR BRAND. SIMPLE, ATTRACTIVE, FULL OF CHARACTER, CLEAN, STRAIGHT TO THE POINT.

Tip #7:

Have a sense of humour. One of the most off-putting characteristics is when people take things or themselves too seriously. Try to lighten up. You don't have to be formal as long as you're not overly presumptuous. Getting to know people should be fun. Just relax and enjoy it.

Tip #8:

VC's & Angels are not your friends, they are your investors. Keep it professional at all times. Relationship is important, but both of you are here for the money. Understand the importance of Protocol, Respect & Professionalism.

Tip #9:
As a Business owner, never, ever take your eyes off your cashflow. Cashflow is the life-blood of every Business. Always know where you stand and where your break-even point is.

Tip #10:

Repeat customers are walking billboards. If a customer comes back to your business, chances are pretty good that he liked what he saw the first time around. Focus on Repeat Customers by making sure the quality of service is consistent enough to keep them coming back.

TIP #II:
LOYALTY IS CRUCIAL. PEOPLE SHOULD WORK
WITH YOU NOT FOR YOU. IT'S THE STRENGTH OF
YOUR TEAM'S ATTITUDE THAT WILL PROPEL
YOUR COMPANY TO UNDISCOVERED HEIGHTS.
WE RESPECT THEM, THEY RESPECT US.
TEAMWORK IS THE BIGGEST PART OF YOUR
ORGANISATION.

TIP #12:

MAKE METRICS MEANINGFUL.

YOU CAN MEASURE THE PERFORMANCE OF YOUR BUSINESS IN A VARIETY OF DIFFERENT WAYS, INCLUDING THINGS LIKE SALES PER VISITOR, AVERAGE ORDER VALUE, REVENUE (AND PROFIT) PER PRODUCT, AND MUCH MORE. MAKE METRICS MEANINGFUL. BUSINESS IS, AND WILL ALWAYS BE, A NUMBERS' GAME.

TIP #13:
CREATE BRAND AMBASSADORS.
BRAND AMBASSADORS ARE EVERYDAY
CUSTOMERS WHO LOVE YOUR PRODUCTS OR
SERVICES SO MUCH THAT THEY JUST CAN'T HELP
BUT TELL EVERYONE THEY MEET ABOUT YOU.
THEY MAY NOT KNOW IT, BUT THEY ARE
IRREPLACEABLE.

TIP #14:
GOOD HABITS ARE THE FOUNDATION OF WEALTH BUILDING. THE MAJOR DIFFERENCE BETWEEN SUCCESSFUL AND UNSUCCESSFUL PEOPLE LIES IN THEIR DAILY HABITS. FIX YOUR DAILY HABITS AND YOU FIX YOUR LIFE!

Tip #15:

If you're serious about cleaning up your finances and getting ahead financially, you must allocate time and energy to updating your budget every week. This will ensure you're not spending more than you earn and that you're able to save towards important financial goals. Create a budget for your company. Create a budget for your personal life. And stick to both religiously.

TIP #16:

SPEND TIME BOILING DOWN WHAT YOUR
BUSINESS IS, WHAT IT DOES, AND WHAT
IT REPRESENTS. IF YOU CAN NAIL DOWN A
60 OR 90 SECOND SYNOPSIS, IT WILL PAY
HUGE DIVIDENDS THROUGHOUT THE
LIFE OF YOUR BUSINESS.

Tip #17:

Check your credit regularly. Your credit report is like a file on you and your credit history. It basically tells lenders how risky a borrower you are. Bad credit is one of the biggest potential roadblocks for business owners. Find out your current credit score, speak to an advisor and get it fixed now.

Tip #18:

Every now and again, turn off your laptop and iPhone, and get out there. Don't sit in front of a screen all day. Switch everything off and venture out into the real world regularly. If you've been neglecting this part of life, start with your own backyard, then expand your field of vision.

Tip #19:
Stay alive. As long as you are alive, anything is still possible.

Tip #20:

Set goals. Winners set goals; losers make excuses. Goals give you more than a reason to get up in the morning; they are an incentive to keep you going all day. They must be measurable, identifiable, obtainable, specific and in writing. Set only three daily major goals and allow room for nothing else to steal your time.

Tip #21:

Become a customer-service fanatic. They say the sale begins when the customer says yes. Good salespeople make sure the job gets done on time — and done right. There's one thing no business has enough of: customers. Take care of the customers you've got (service & value), and they'll take care of you (money & referrals). You must have a fanatical attention to detail.

Tip #22:

Make sure your product or service idea is a must-have idea, not a nice-to-have one. A lot of "new ideas" end up being utter nonsense. Most ideas can be turned into selling products, but you won't end up building a business out of them. These ideas are the nice-to-have ones. Spend time getting to know (from the market) whether your idea or product or service is a nice-to-have or a must-have. It will save you so much time, money and energy.

TIP #23:
KEEP YOUR USP AS UNIQUE AS POSSIBLE SO THAT YOU DETERMINE THE PRICING YOURSELF. IF THE MARKET YOU'RE ENTERING IS TOO WIDE, YOU'LL SUFFER CASHFLOW-WISE AND WILL BE FORCED TO COMPETE IN PRICE. TO GAIN MARKET SHARE, YOU HAVE TO STRATEGISE AND NOT WASTE TIME OR ENERGY COMPETING WITH THE BIG GUNS. LEAVE WORLD DOMINATION TO THE OLD MASTERS, FIND YOUR NICHE AND WORK TOWARDS THAT NICHE DOMINATION INSTEAD.

TIP #24:

MAKE SURE YOU'VE GOT A WEBSITE THAT
SERVES A REAL PURPOSE. BUSINESSES OFTEN
MISTAKENLY TREAT THEIR WEBSITES LIKE AN
INTERACTIVE BUSINESS CARD. THEIR SITES
ALLOW PEOPLE TO CLICK THROUGH PERTINENT
INFORMATION ABOUT THE BIZ, BUT BEYOND
THAT, THERE'S NO REAL PURPOSE TO THE SITE.
SO HERE'S THE KEY: PRETEND YOUR WEBSITE IS
A HOUSE. DON'T JUST LET YOUR GUESTS WALK
AROUND WITHOUT KNOWING WHERE TO SIT OR
PUT DOWN THEIR STUFF. HOST YOUR GUESTS.
MAKE THEM WANNA STAY. BE HOSPITABLE.

TIP #25:

WEAR HEADPHONES. HEADPHONES CAN HELP SHUT OUT DISTRACTIONS AND KEEP YOU FOCUSED. MUSIC IS GOOD. MUSIC CAN INSPIRE PRODUCTIVITY. MORE MOZART & MILES DAVIS, LESS KANYE WEST & KAIZER CHIEFS.

Tip #26:

Wake up at an ungodly hour to achieve godly duties. To really get stuff done, you've got to get up in time to make it happen. Start with prayer, meditation, or whatever feeds your spirit and soul. Anytime from 5:30 to 7:00 a.m is ideal. If your morning routine takes a little longer, bring your wake-up time back a little more. Adjust your bedtime accordingly and place your alarm device across the room.

Tip #27:
Don't hold meetings (even over the phone). If you've been in business for very long, you should know by now that most meetings are a waste of time. Avoid meetings if at all possible.
Keep them at a minimum.

Tip #28:

Validate your idea. Your idea is absolutely worthless if you keep it to yourself and do not test it with actual customers. Go to Starbucks and offer to buy a coffee for whoever will give your idea or new concept a fair & honest evaluation. Share it with as many people as possible and get real human opinion & advice on it.

Tip #29:

Stay energetic. Starting a successful business requires tireless enthusiasm and boundless stores of positive energy. You simply HAVE to be excited about the product or service you're providing. If you're not super excited, no one else will be. On the flip side, enthusiasm is infectious. Your excitement will help you secure business leads and build a committed, energetic team.

Tip #30:

Value people and nurture relationships. Top-notch people skills are vital to sound leadership. Develop premium listening, communication and decision-making skill sets. Demonstrate integrity by being open, honest and fair. Learn to really listen to people. It's just nice. be nice.

TIP #31:

DELIVER ON RESULTS PROMISED. DON'T BE A TALKER. BE A DOER. ABLE LEADERSHIP REQUIRES AN ABILITY TO DELIVER RESULTS. REMEMBER TO FOLLOW UP AND FOLLOW THROUGH. ENGAGE EXPERTS IF NECESSARY TO TIMELY AND COMPETENTLY PULL PROJECTS FORWARD. IN THE END, ONLY SUBSTANCE AND THE FINAL SUM WILL MATTER. EXCUSES WON'T.

T<small>IP</small> #32:
H<small>AVE REGULAR SHARED MEALS WITH YOUR</small>
<small>TEAM.</small> E<small>ATING REGULARLY WITH YOUR TEAM</small>
<small>ALLOWS FOR CASUAL CONVERSATION IN A</small>
<small>COMFORTABLE ENVIRONMENT, LETTING TEAM</small>
<small>MEMBERS GET TO KNOW EACH OTHER OUTSIDE</small>
<small>OF WORK.</small> T<small>HIS IS VERY IMPORTANT FOR</small>
<small>CREATING GOOD COMPANY CULTURE.</small>

Tip #33:

Do the math: Find 200 people willing to pay £100 each for something and you just grew your business' revenue by £20,000. Layer in product sales, consulting contracts and sponsorships, and pretty soon that rapid revenue growth begins to look quite impressive. Think, think, think.

Tip #34:
The Harder and Smarter you work,
the More you will Earn.
Simple.

Tip #35:

Stop thinking about making a million and start thinking about serving a million people. When you only have a few customers and your goal is to make a lot of money, you're forced to find ways to wring every last dollar out of those customers. When you find a way to serve a million people, many other benefits follow. Wanna make a million pounds right now? Create a valuable product that costs £1 and sell it to a million people who will constantly need it.

Tip #36:

As a business owner, focus on this: Do one thing better, one thing at a time. Pick one thing you're already better at than most people. Just. One. Thing. Become maniacally focused at doing that one thing. Work. Train. Learn. Practice. Evaluate. Refine. Get better.

Tip #37:

Work out all kinks before thinking of expanding. As entrepreneurs, we all have a "bigger picture" that we are shooting for, but it is important that you don't put the cart before the horse, especially when it comes to expansion. All growth must be strategic. Master crawling before walking or running. Nothing is more important than a well-laid foundation.

TIP #38:
FIND A GOOD LAWYER. A GREAT ONE.
PARTNERING WITH A TRUSTWORTHY ATTORNEY
WHO IS KNOWLEDGEABLE AND SAVVY IN
HELPING ENTREPRENEURS IS PIVOTAL. IT WILL
ALWAYS BE WORTH THE MONEY.

Tip #39:

Figure out your burn rate.
This is how much money it costs to keep
your business running each month.
Keep this number as close to
very low as you can. Map out
your monthly expenses on a visible
calendar. Be aware of what's
happening to your money.

Tip #40:

Ask for terms on everything. Stretch out your money to build your business. Hold on to it for as long as you can. Learn the art of negotiation and never allow a salesman to swindle you. If you leave a store feeling like you overpaid on something, you definitely did. Gut feelings never lie.

TIP #41:
MEASURE PASSION. SKILLS AND TALENT
ARE IMPORTANT, BUT YOU MUST ALSO TAKE
INTO ACCOUNT WHETHER CANDIDATES
ARE PASSIONATE ABOUT GOING TO WORK
FOR YOU AND WITH YOU.

TIP #42:
INTERVIEW LIKE A PRO. WHETHER IN PERSON OR OVER THE INTERNET OR OVER THE PHONE, MAKE SURE YOU GET THE INTERVIEW RIGHT. PREPARE INSIGHTFUL QUESTIONS AND FOCUS MORE ON CHARACTER AND PASSION RATHER THAN EXPERIENCE AND EXPERTISE. AN INEXPERIENCED FUTURE LONG-TERM ADVOCATE IS BETTER THAN AN EXPERIENCED SHORT TERM KNOW-IT-ALL. SHOW UP ON TIME, BE POSITIVE, AND DILIGENTLY ADDRESS ANY RED FLAGS YOU MAY HAVE FOUND ON A RESUME.

Tip #43:

Practice your elevator pitch. Your elevator pitch is critical today in a wide variety of contexts. It's the short bio you use each time you have a chance to advertise or promote what you do. It's the 10 second pitch you use when meeting a prospective client or a potential new associate at a networking event. It's how you describe what you do at an investor pitch panel. Perfect it, and be prepared always.

TIP #44:
DON'T FORGET PR. TRADITIONAL AND ONLINE PRESS RELATIONS CAN YIELD COVERAGE THAT HAS LONGER SHELF LIFE AND COSTS LESS THAN ADVERTISING. THINK ABOUT WHAT MAKES YOUR PRODUCT NEW, INTERESTING, AND RELEVANT. THEN, TALK TO THE MEDIA ABOUT IT. YOU MIGHT GET GREAT REVIEWS, MENTIONS ON BLOGS, OR EVEN APPEAR ON NEWS SEGMENTS. MANY MEDIA OUTLETS HAVE SECTIONS DEDICATED TO PEOPLE IN THE COMMUNITY DOING OUTSTANDING THINGS. EVEN AN ARTICLE IN A UNIVERSITY CAMPUS NEWSPAPER CAN BE A VALUABLE SOURCE OF PUBLICITY.

TIP #45:

READ CUSTOMER EMAILS. IF ANYTHING, IT HUMBLES YOU. YOU THINK YOU UNDERSTAND YOUR CUSTOMERS...BUT DO YOU? EVEN TIM COOK, HEAD OF THE WORLD'S MOST VALUABLE COMPANY, CARVES OUT TIME TO WALK AROUND COMPANY STORES & READ CUSTOMER E-MAILS.

Tip #46:

Read before you write or work. Reading a good book will get your creative juices flowing, your brain learning, and your knowledge base growing. Try reading for 30 minutes to start your day. Readers will always and forever be leaders. Fall in love with learning.

TIP #47:
PUT YOUR FAMILY FIRST. SUCCESS CAN'T
EXIST WITHOUT FAMILY — EVEN IF THAT
"FAMILY" IS SIMPLY LOVED ONES & FRIENDS.
YOU NEED TO BE WORKING FOR A
GREATER PURPOSE THAN YOUR OWN
MONETARY GAIN IF YOU'RE GOING TO
ACCOMPLISH TRUE SUCCESS.

TIP #48:
WAKE UP EARLY TO WORK. THE LIST OF
SUCCESSFUL PEOPLE WHO WAKE UP BEFORE THE
REST OF THE WORLD IS FAR TOO LONG TO LIST.
THIS ISN'T A COINCIDENCE. GET UP BEFORE
7AM, 7 DAYS A WEEK (YES, INCLUDING
WEEKENDS) AND GET A HEAD START ON YOUR
DAY AND YOUR DREAM. TRY TO WAKE UP AT THE
SAME TIME EVERYDAY. HAVING A GOOD SLEEP
ROUTINE WILL HELP YOU HAVE MORE ENERGY TO
DO MORE WORK DURING THE DAY.

Tip #49:

Always, always, always have a small pocket notebook on you. You've probably heard the classic tale of someone who wakes in the middle of the night with a great idea, goes back to sleep, and forgets it by morning. You want that notebook with you at all times, because you never know when inspiration might strike.

Tip #50:

Never use your credit card to buy things you cannot afford. Living a borrowed lifestyle is the quickest way to get into debt. If you can't afford a purchase today, chances are you won't be able to afford it tomorrow, or even next month. Don't fall into the category of fake entrepreneurs who are obsessed with looking good and not actually being good. You will get caught out.

Tip #51:

Always present a proposal in writing. People do not believe what they hear, they believe what they see. Always have a contract available and a writing pad. Anything offered or points of value that are included should be written down to show buyers what they get when they make a decision with you.

Tip #52:

Learn to raise capital by any means necessary. That's your primary job as an entrepreneur. To bring value to the world and make money. lots of money. You must continually raise capital from family & friends, banks, suppliers, customers and investors. Be a serial capital raiser.

Tip #53:

Don't wait till you are big before you begin building your brand. Build your brand from scratch alongside building your business. Both go hand in hand.

TIP #54:
CREATE MULTIPLE FLOWS OF INCOME. THE REALLY RICH NEVER DEPEND ON ONE FLOW OF INCOME BUT INSTEAD CREATE A NUMBER OF REVENUE STREAMS. ONCE YOU HAVE ONE BUSINESS ESTABLISHED AND RUNNING SMOOTHLY, GET THE NEXT ONE SET IN MOTION. AND DIVERSIFY, DO NOT OPEN SIMILAR STYLES OF BUSINESS ALL AT ONCE. IT WILL WEAR YOU THIN.

Tip #55:

Use cloud-based financial apps for the management and organisation of your money. Make your financial life easier with simple online tools such as Expensify, Udemy, Quickbooks, Wave, InDinero, FreshBooks and Teaspiller.

TIP #56:
BECOME FINANCIALLY LITERATE. LEARN TO MASTER YOUR MONEY OR IT WILL MASTER YOU. IT'S AN IMPORTANT SKILL TO BE ABLE TO CLOSELY MONITOR EXPENSES AND GAIN A WORKING KNOWLEDGE OF YOUR BASIC SMALL BUSINESS FINANCIAL STATEMENTS.

Tip #57:

THE BEST WAY TO GAIN THE MOST EXPOSURE FOR YOUR SMALL BUSINESS IS VIA SOCIAL MEDIA MARKETING, WHICH OFFERS THE ADDITIONAL BENEFIT OF BEING FREE. CREATE ACCOUNTS ON FACEBOOK & TWITTER AND POST HELPFUL AND VALUABLE CONTENT TO YOUR POTENTIAL CUSTOMERS. MAKE THE EXPERIENCE AS INTERACTIVE AS POSSIBLE BY PERSONALLY REPLYING TO EACH PERSON WHO RESPONDS. ONCE YOUR POPULARITY BEGINS TO GROW, CONSIDER CONDUCTING WEEKLY TWEETCHATS ON TOPICS RELEVANT TO YOUR BUSINESS, AND OFFER GIVEAWAYS TO BOOST YOUR PRESENCE ON FACEBOOK.

Tip #58:

Create a clear model of your sales funnel, then invest in top-quality analytics to see how your customers proceed through that funnel. Sales is a numbers game, so you need data to know how your business is really performing.

TIP #59:

A FANCY SITE IS NICE, BUT NO ONE WILL EVER SEE IT IF IT TAKES MINUTES TO FULLY LOAD. DIGITAL AUDIENCES ARE IMPATIENT AND WILL NOT HESITATE TO BOUNCE, FINDING THEIR WAY OUT OF A WEBSITE'S PROVERBIAL DOOR. FOCUS SOLELY ON YOUR WEBSITE'S QUALITY, CLARITY, USER-FRIENDLINESS & PERFORMANCE. THERE'S NO EXCUSE FOR A BADLY RUN WEBSITE.

Tip #60:

As an entrepreneur with a new business idea, you may think you've zeroed in on a perfect business plan but you'll need to learn to take in the opinions of others. Then if it appears that your plan won't work, then adjust. Be open-minded.

TIP #61:

GIVE BACK. WHETHER IT'S TO A CHARITY, A CAUSE YOU BELIEVE IN OR A STRANGER WHO COULD BENEFIT FROM YOUR HELP, THERE ARE IMMEASURABLE BENEFITS TO THINKING OF OTHERS. FOR ONE, YOU'LL BECOME A BETTER AND MORE ATTENTIVE PERSON. YOU'LL FOCUS LESS ON YOUR OWN SHORTCOMINGS AND BECOME A MORE GENEROUS CONTRIBUTOR TO SOCIETY. FEW THINGS ARE BETTER THAN THIS.

TIP #62:
ESTABLISH AN EMERGENCY FUND FOR YOUR BUSINESS. AN EMERGENCY FUND IS A CASH CUSHION THAT WILL SUPPORT YOUR LIVING EXPENSES FOR AT LEAST 3 MONTHS. IT CAN ALSO COME IN HANDY WHEN YOU NEED TO COVER UNFORESEEN EXPENSES IN YOUR EVERYDAY LIFE SUCH AS REPAIRS, MEDICAL EXPENSES AND OTHER EMERGENCIES.

Tip #63:

Simplify Your Life. Life is becoming more complex with almost every passing day. Running after money and your financial goals will distract you from things that are very important in life. Sometimes less is definitely more.

Tip #64:

Learn from your competitors. Know what it is that they do well and what areas they can improve on. It's good to have your eyes and ears on your surroundings. It's not just survival of the fittest...it's survival of the smartest too.

Tip #65:

Always think about the logistics. It's not enough to have an amazing idea — the key to success is in how you execute it.

Tip #66:

Thoroughly research the market you will be selling in before you even think of going into it. Never underestimate the importance of knowing who your customers are and what they really want from you.

Tip #67:

When closing, remain seated. Most sales companies will say present the product, service or idea on your feet, but always negotiate from your seat. Even if your prospect stands up, remain seated. Going from a seating position to standing up suggests something has changed and allows your prospect to exit and end the negotiations. When it comes to one on one in (and out of) person sales, easy does it, remain calm and in control.

Tip #68:

Always treat prospects like buyers. Regardless of the circumstances of the individual in question: no money, no budget, not the decision maker – always treat the prospect like he or she is a certified buyer.

Tip #69:

Don't define success with a dollar amount, but in relation to your happiness. The habit of defining success with a dollar amount will lead you to constantly chasing Money. It's a chase that will never end, and a view of success that will never be attained. Get in the habit of seeing your success and your happiness in the same light. Be content. You can love making money but you don't need to love money itself.

TIP #70:
BUY A WHITEBOARD.
USE A BIG WHITEBOARD TO KEEP
YOUR GOALS VISIBLE AND CLOSE.
WHITEBOARDS ARE GOOD TO HAVE.

Tip #71:

Always learn to make eye contact when speaking to people. This is a discipline instilled only through practice, and you can perfect it by recording yourself. I f you want to be believed, it is vital to make eye contact with your prospect. Never trust anyone who struggles to maintain eye contact with you.

TIP #72:

DISCUSS THINGS WITH YOUR STAFF REGULARLY (THIS DOESN'T MEAN CONSTANTLY MEET WITH THEM). YOU MIGHT BE THINKING ABOUT YOUR BUSINESS ALL THE TIME, BUT IT'S EASY TO NOT KNOW HOW TO PROPERLY COMMUNICATE YOUR THOUGHTS WITH STAFF. YOU MIGHT HAVE CHANGED THE COMPANY'S DIRECTION OR ADDED SERVICES WITHOUT BRINGING EVERYONE TO THE TABLE. WE ALL DESIRE TO BE INVOLVED, LET YOUR STAFF IN WHEN IT'S APPROPRIATE.

Tip #73:

Seriously and realistically evaluate your company's level of technology. Even if you work by yourself. When you review the year or the month or even the week, be aware of how you and your staffers have used existing systems. Probably members of your team live and die by certain software programs but use others infrequently. Sometimes if employees aren't using a certain software program, a system or a piece of equipment, they don't understand it. Evaluate and get feedback on what works and what doesn't.

Tip #74:
Word of wisdom: Quality is more important than quantity. One home run is much better than two doubles. Chew on that for a while.

Tip #75:

Pick your partners wisely. Founding a company with someone is a lot like getting married to them. You're going to be spending a LOT of time with this person so make sure you like them, trust them, and believe in them and that they feel the same about you. If you don't, you can always try to change that at a later date, but it's better if you gel from the start.

Tip #76:

80% OF YOUR SALES COME FROM ONLY 20% OF YOUR CUSTOMERS. THIS IS SIMPLY FACT FOR ALMOST ALL BUSINESSES. THIS MEANS YOU NEED TO MAKE IT A PRIORITY TO FIND OUT WHICH ONE IN FIVE OF YOUR CUSTOMERS ARE THOSE WHO KEEP COMING BACK FOR MORE OF WHAT YOU HAVE TO OFFER. PAY ATTENTION, FIND OUT WHO THEY ARE, AND THEN MAKE EVERY EFFORT TO KEEP THEM HAPPY AND ALWAYS BUYING.

Tip #77:

Exercise. Exercise. Exercise. Scientific evidence shows that morning exercise can make us think better, work better, and become more productive. A morning spin cycle class, quick jog or 30-minute yoga or pilates session can prepare you for a powerful session of getting stuff done and making some serious money. Make it a rule to break a sweat everyday, regardless of your "busy" schedule.

TIP #78:

DON'T COMMUTE. IF YOU TYPICALLY HAVE A LENGTHY WORK COMMUTE, DO EVERYTHING YOU CAN TO REDUCE THE DURATION OF IT. IT'S NOT JUST WASTED TIME THAT YOU WANT TO GUARD AGAINST. IT'S THE MENTAL HAVOC. A COMMUTE IS ONE OF THE MOST STRESSFUL PARTS OF THE DAY. STARTING YOUR WORKDAY WITH THAT LEVEL OF STRESS CAN COMPLETELY RUIN YOUR PRODUCTIVITY. DON'T EVEN COMMUTE TO STARBUCKS. HAVE STARBUCKS BRING COFFEE TO YOU INSTEAD.

Tip #79:

Eavesdrop to find the social butterflies. Use Twitter to gauge the pulse of the local conversation and make a contribution. You'll be shocked how easily accepting the world of Twitter, Facebook and Periscope is. If you have something to say, the world is ready to listen.

TIP #80:
PERFECTION IS THE ENEMY OF
PROGRESS. REMEMBER PERFECTION ISN'T
NECESSARY TO RUN A SUCCESSFUL
PROFITABLE BUSINESS.
CONSISTENCY AND LONGEVITY IS.

TIP #81:

HAVE DINNER WITH INTERESTING PEOPLE. TARGET INVESTORS AND POTENTIAL CLIENTS AND TREAT THEM TO GOOD THINGS. PAY FOR CINEMA TICKETS. BUY BOX SEATS TO A BIG SPORTS GAME COMING UP. GO THE EXTRA MILE. DO WHATEVER IT WILL TAKE TO GRAB THEIR ATTENTION AND YOU WILL BE THE FIRST NAME THAT COMES OUT OF THEIR MOUTHS. SOLIDIFY RELATIONSHIPS AND ALWAYS, ALWAYS, ALWAYS TRY TO IMPRESS.

Tip #82:

Establish an impeccable standard of excellence. Always. It doesn't matter how much it costs, work towards and maintain a flawless level of excellence. It's rule 101 for every SuperEntrepreneur.

Tip #83:

Have a team of both extroverts and introverts. It's good to have a nice mix of personalities and characters. That way, you can choose which side to go to when you have both good days and bad days.

Tip #84:

Delegate and trust that others can rise to the occasion. Learn to let go of control. Sometimes seizing the reins is appropriate but on other occasions relinquishing control over employees can benefit everyone. Learn to trust your team to do the hard stuff. That's the only way they will grow.

Tip #85:

There exists only one unbreakable rule for entrepreneurial growth: Get revenue! That's it. There are a thousand tasks that compete for your attention every day, but raising revenue must always remain at the top of your list. If you're not making money, it doesn't make any sense.

TIP #86:
HAVE VERY TOUGH SKIN. AND WHEN YOU THINK IT'S TOUGH ENOUGH, DEVELOP SOME MORE. PEOPLE WILL BE PEOPLE. SOME WILL LOVE WHAT YOU HAVE TO OFFER, SOME WILL ABSOLUTELY HATE IT AND DISREGARD IT. THAT'S LIFE. REJECTION WILL COME REGULARLY AND THERE WILL BE PLENTY OF LITTLE (AND BIG) FAILURES. AT TIMES, IT WILL TAKE SHEER WILLPOWER TO MOVE FORWARD. THIS MAKES IT ALL THAT MUCH SWEETER IN THE END.

Tip #87:

They're right – it truly is all about the customer. Without happy customers, profit margins can never increase. When trying to build a name and brand, it is critical to go above and beyond for customers. This is especially critical in the beginning years as the business grows its customer base.

Tip #88:

Monitor your breakeven and key numbers. The most important day of the month is the day that you break even and start making a profit. If you don't know which day of the month that is, you need to find out today. Knowing both the date and the amount allows you to monitor your performance and take measures to correct issues right away. Waiting until the end of the year for your accountant to produce financial statements is not a good idea — if you are behind, you need to know now so that you can correct the situation.

TIP #89:

IT'S OK TO SAY NO. KNOW WHEN TO WALK AWAY FROM A CANDIDATE WHEN YOU KNOW YOU DON'T HAVE THE RIGHT PERSON. DON'T SETTLE FOR SOMEONE WHO YOU FEEL IN YOUR GUT YOU MIGHT HAVE TO LET GO IN TWO OR THREE MONTHS. IT ISN'T GOOD FOR YOU, THE COMPANY OR THE CANDIDATE.

TIP #90:
PROTECT YOUR BRAND. PROTECT YOUR END-GAME VISION. JOINING FORCES WITH A PARTNER TAKES A LOT OF ENERGY, AND CHANCES ARE THAT SOMEWHERE DOWN THE LINE YOU WILL LOSE YOUR FOCUS. WORKING FOR A COMMON GOAL WITHIN A NEW TEAM IS REALLY EXCITING BUT MERGING FORCES DOES NOT NECESSARILY MEAN MERGING IDENTITIES. KEEP THINGS EXCLUSIVE.

TIP #91:
CLEAN YOUR DIET UP. DON'T BE ADDICTED TO
JUNK FOOD. PIZZAS AND KEBABS ARE COOL BUT
KEEP IT AT A MINIMUM, ESPECIALLY DURING
THOSE LATE WORK ALL-NIGHTERS. FILLING
YOUR DIET WITH LEAN MEATS, FISH, NUTS,
LOADS OF WATER, FRUITS & VEG IS THE TRUE
WAY TO A HEALTHIER LIFE.

TIP #92:
USE SOCIAL MEDIA FOR EARLY MARKETING. HIRE A PROFESSIONAL MARKETING AND PUBLIC RELATIONS AGENCY ONCE YOU HAVE A GOOD REVENUE STREAM BUT YOU DON'T NEED THEM TO START A FREE BLOG, ESTABLISH FACEBOOK AND TWITTER ACCOUNTS WITH INITIAL CONTENT OR COMPLETE THE BASICS OF SEARCH ENGINE OPTIMISATION (SEO). YOU CAN DO ALL THAT YOURSELF. SOCIAL MEDIA IS NOT ROCKET SCIENCE, IT JUST TAKES A BIT OF LEARNING AND OPENING UP YOUR MIND A BIT.

Tip #93:

Visit and use as many free online learning sites as possible. Learning the new skills necessary to start a new business can be expensive, but fortunately the initiative for free, high-quality, educational resources online has only continued to grow in the past few years. Get familiar with sites like Codeacademy, LearnVest, OpenCulture, Coursera, Khan Academy and even Youtube and grasp the fundamentals of running a business, selling and the intricacies of your industry.

Tip #94:

Review your profit and loss statements, balance sheet, income statements and general ledger for accuracy and ensure that all transactions have been recorded. Make sure the bank and credit card accounts are reconciled and that loan interest has been separated from the principal and is accurately logged onto your books. Always check the accuracy of accounts receivable and accounts payable. Write off bad debt for customers when necessary. Get hands-on. Learn how to do this, don't leave everything to your business accountant. What you do not know has the ability to kill your business.

TIP #95:

HOLIDAY PARTIES ARE 100 PERCENT DEDUCTIBLE. IF YOU HOLD A PARTY FOR YOUR STAFF – IN YOUR FACILITY OR AT A RESTAURANT – YOU CAN DEDUCT ALL OF THE COST IN THIS INSTANCE. AS LONG AS THE PARTY IS FOR THE BENEFIT OF EMPLOYEES AND IS NOT LIMITED TO THE TOP BRASS, YOU CAN WRITE OFF 100 PERCENT OF YOUR COSTS. IMPORTANT INFORMATION, IF YOU ASK ME.

Tip #96:

Have a dedicated business account and business credit card. If your business account is low on funds, it's easier to account for making a loan to your business than it is to account for business expenses paid from a personal account.

More Tips for The SuperEntrepreneur

Narrow minds and wide mouths are often together. Be careful.

Every person you meet is a teacher and every environment you find yourself in is a classroom.

Know more than others. Work more than others. Risk more than others.

80% of success is just showing up.

You are in control of your reality. Nobody else is.

Build your network. Your network is truly going to affect your future net worth.

Be specific. Be a copycat. Keep things simple.

Solve your own problems before solving others. You can't fill anyone else's cup with an empty jug.

Think outside the box. Travel. Explore. Live.

The idea itself is 1%. The other 99% is execution.

If you want to succeed in business, you need adaptability, creativity & grit. Lots of it!

Be fearless. Take no prisoners. If you want to succeed, then succeed! Who's permission are you waiting for?!

The biggest risk in business is to purely driven by emotion.

Surround yourself with hungry people. Hungry people win.

Only 44% of new businesses survive the 1st year. Don't be so relaxed. Get to work. Fight against that statistic.

Analyse your budget, balance sheets and use your income statement to attack financial flaws, mistakes and weaknesses.

Durable, affordable, exclusive, on time, high quality, unique. These are necessary characteristics of your product and service.

Take chances. Make smart choices but take necessary risks.

Plan ahead. Emails, calls, documents, meetings. Plan ahead.

Be at the right place at the right time. Meet people.

MONEYSMARTS: THE BUSINESS OF BUSINESS

"BUSINESS OPPORTUNITIES ARE LIKE BUSES, THERE'S ALWAYS ANOTHER ONE COMING." – RICHARD BRANSON, FOUNDER OF VIRGIN GROUP

TIP #97:

TAKE ACTIVE BREAKS. A WORK BREAK SHOULD
ENHANCE YOUR WORKING EXPERIENCE NOT TAKE
AWAY FROM IT. DO SOMETHING ACTIVE THAT
WILL GET YOUR BLOOD PUMPING AND YOUR MIND
WORKING AS EFFECTIVELY AS IT WAS WHEN YOU
FIRST STARTED WORKING IN THE EARLY HOURS
OF THE MORNING.

Tip #98:

Tell the truth. It may sound cliché, but if you always tell the truth, you never have to remember what you've said. In business and in life, cutting corners catches up with you, ALWAYS. No-one wants to do business with a liar. Integrity & honesty are very important and have critical ramifications.

Tip #99:

Hire the right people. Never skimp on getting the best people...for you, not just for the business. You want people who will learn, teach, understand and synergise with you easily. Since your employees are on the front line, their demeanour & interaction with clients can cement relationships that bring customers back to your business. Finding individuals who are positive, friendly & really care about doing a great job is the first step. Anyone who is going to interact with customers—from the receptionist through to the collections department—has to understand the importance of creating a positive interaction with the customer.

"IF YOU HAVE AN EXIT STRATEGY, IT'S NOT AN OBSESSION."
-MARK CUBAN, BILLIONAIRE

TIP #100:
KNOW THAT 80% OF YOUR SALES COME FROM 20% OF YOUR CUSTOMERS. THIS IS A FACT FOR ALMOST ALL BUSINESSES. THIS MEANS YOU NEED TO MAKE IT A PRIORITY TO FIND OUT WHICH ONE IN FIVE OF YOUR CUSTOMERS ARE THOSE WHO KEEP COMING BACK FOR MORE OF WHAT YOU HAVE TO OFFER AND THEN MAKE EVERY EFFORT TO KEEP THEM HAPPY AND BUYING.

Tip #101:

Keep it personal. By definition, a repeat customer is someone you get to know. Nurture that by keeping your relationship as personal as possible. Get to know your customers by name. And it's Mr. Davidson, not John. Keep it personal yes, but never compromise your level of professionalism and decorum. (I love the word decorum). …Decorum. Decorum. It just sounds good.

Tip #102:

Always have good people on the ground but send out your best talent if you have to. Your people are core to the success of your business; They are the ones who know the complete business model & company culture inside out. Decide to plant your best individuals in overseas markets rather than rely on headhunters & outside recruitment agencies. Nothing beats home-grown talent.

TIP #103:

NEVER ASSUME YOU KNOW HOW TO BRAND AND MARKET YOUR PRODUCT IN OVERSEAS TERRITORIES AND NEVER ASSUME YOU KNOW EXACTLY WHO YOUR CUSTOMER WILL BE WHEN YOU GO OVERSEAS. DIFFERENT COUNTRY, DIFFERENT RULES. LISTEN TO YOUR COLLABORATORS AND LEARN FROM THEM.

Tip #104:

If you want to provide a quick and open dialogue with customers, micro-blogging, using a platform like Twitter is a very good option. Engage with the world through 140 characters.

Tip #105:

If your business lends itself to frequent customers queries and there are no existing discussion forums, consider hosting a forum on your website or at least on a Facebook page. By doing this, You become the go-to place for potential clients to vent frustrations & complaints, discuss innovations & market updates and share ideas & new insights. If this is happening anywhere, it should be on your platform. This can massively boost your reputation as a market or industry leader.

TIP #106:

MARKETPLACES ARE IN CONSTANT FLUX. MEANING NEW TRENDS TAKE SHAPE, CONSUMER HABITS CHANGE, FRESH COMPETITORS EMERGE, TECHNOLOGY CHANGES THE WAY BUSINESSES OPERATE – ARE YOU ALIVE TO THESE CHANGES? BE ALIVE TO THESE CHANGES. OBSESS OVER YOUR INDUSTRY.

TIP #107:
WHETHER YOU'RE PLANNING TO GROW OR
CONSOLIDATE THE BUSINESS YOU'VE BUILT SO
FAR, THE RIGHT PREMISES IS A VITAL PLATFORM
AND A BIG DIFFERENCE MAKER. ASK YOURSELF
THIS: DOES MY PREMISES MATCH MY AMBITION?
AM I THINKING BIG ENOUGH?

Tip #108:

Do your homework on taxes. If you are selling to non-UK businesses in the EU and they are registered for VAT in their own country, they can quote their VAT registration number in order to be exempt from VAT. It's essential that you accept this and know this. Be aware what overseas customers may have to pay when they buy from you. Very few entrepreneurs take time out to learn about taxes. Do your homework on taxes or be ready to lose money in the long run.

"TO BE A SUCCESSFUL
MANAGER, ATTITUDE AND
ABILITY ARE EQUALLY
IMPORTANT INGREDIENTS. A
LEADER INSPIRES OTHERS TO
GREATNESS. A BOSS DOMINATES
HIS SUBORDINATES AND MAKES
THEM FEEL SMALL."
- LI KA-SHING,
ASIAN BILLIONAIRE

TIP #109:

IF YOU WANT CUSTOMERS TO KEEP COMING BACK
AND BUYING FROM YOU, THEN YOU NEED TO
EARN THAT LOYALTY. MOST PEOPLE ARE
LOOKING FOR TRUST IN A SUPPLIER.
CAN YOU BE TRUSTED AND HOW DO YOU
ACTIVELY DEMONSTRATE THAT TRUST?
THINK VIRGIN ATLANTIC.

Tip #110:

If you want to attract customers based on exclusivity, focus on innovation. Offer something no-one else can copy. Do things differently if you want different results. Sometimes it's better to apologise for breaking the rules than to ask for permission to change them. Think Apple.

Tip #III:

If you have staff, consider how they can help manage your social media marketing. You don't necessarily have to do everything yourself and staff may be able to add some character to your social media activities for you. But keep the boundaries between business and personal communication very very clear.

Tip #112:
FUNDAMENTAL TO YOUR MARKETING STRATEGY IS IDENTIFYING THE TYPE OF CUSTOMER THAT YOU WANT TO HAVE AND TARGETING THEM PRECISELY. ALDI & WAITROSE HAVE VERY DIFFERENT TARGET CUSTOMERS AND THIS SHOWS IN THEIR DIFFERENT LEVELS OF SERVICE AND EVEN THEIR MARKETING STRATEGY. EVEN THOUGH IT'S CRUCIAL TO TRY TO PROVIDE EXTRA BENEFITS TO YOUR CUSTOMERS, REMEMBER THIS: YOU CAN NOT, AND WILL NOT EVER PLEASE EVERYONE. MAKE A CHOICE.

Tip #113:

Respond to customer contact quickly and efficiently. This is rule 101-101 when it comes to customer interaction. This will make them feel their feedback is and acted upon. Never underestimate the power of speed.

Tip #114:

Using social media is primarily an investment in time. And it takes time for your presence to spread across the web. So be patient. Keep a close eye on how it is working for you, but don't lose heart if it doesn't transform your marketing strategy overnight. Stay with it.

Tip #115:

Learn the value of having a strong CPA on your team. This stands for certified public accountant. The right one isn't just your accountant, he or she can be a partner and can become an important extension of your business. Don't just hire anyone, make sure they are certified.

Tip #116:

Your organisation should have some form of governing document, setting out what its purpose is and how it operates: for example, how decisions are taken. In many cases a constitution is a legal requirement (eg if you are a limited company). If your organisation is a charity, you must comply with charity law: for example, ensuring that funds are used only for the charitable purposes set out in your governing document. If your organisation is a company, you must comply with company law (for example, making a company annual return to Companies House). Stick to the rules always.

Tip #117:

You are legally required to pay employers' National Insurance contributions, and to deduct employees' National Insurance contributions and income tax from their pay. Operating PAYE can get really complicated and time-consuming sometimes, so you may want to purchase payroll software or use a payroll service to do it. Look out for software such as MiraclePay, Quickbooks and Sage and get familiar with them.

TIP #118:
ARRANGE FOR REGULAR CHARITABLE GIVING FOR ONE OF TWO GOOD REASONS: THE SELFISH REASONS OF A TAX WRITE-OFF OR FOR GOOD PUBLICITY. OR MAYBE YOU CAN DO SO UNSELFISHLY BECAUSE YOU'RE JUST AN AWESOME PERSON. BUT TAKE TIME TO CONTRIBUTE SOMETHING. CONSIDER LINKING EMPLOYEE GIFTS TO A CHARITY THAT'S ENGAGED IN A SIMILAR AREA TO YOUR COMPANY. MAKING A DONATION OF YOUR TIME OR MONEY HELPS BUILD A SENSE OF PURPOSE FOR YOUR STAFF AND YOUR COMPANY. IT'S GOOD TO BE GOOD.

Tip #119:

Love what you do and become completely obsessed with every aspect of your business. If not, you will get burnt out quickly, which will lead to failure. There is nothing more rewarding than doing something you absolutely love. Do only what you love. Money will never equal happiness.

Tip #120:

Never ever deprive yourself of a benefit. Once you start depriving yourself, you lose the true essence of being an entrepreneur. The entrepreneurial life is a life of financial freedom. Don't allow any purchase or desire to elude you. Pay for it, and go ahead and make TEN times more money than you made previously in order to replace what has been spent or used. You are in control of your financial destiny. Never be afraid or reluctant to treat yourself. Only fixed income earners live that way. It's a poverty constraint. And we don't do poverty at MoneySmarts. We don't like poverty.

TIP #121:

YOUR JOB AS AN ENTREPRENEUR IS TO CREATE A 80% RIGHT PRODUCT AND GET IT OUT INTO THE HANDS OF YOUR CUSTOMERS. YOUR CUSTOMERS WILL TELL YOU THE REST. YOUR CLIENT WILL GET YOU THE EXTRA 20%.

TIP #122:
YOU CAN TURN 5% PROFIT MARGINS INTO 20% PROFIT MARGINS IF YOU'LL JUST HUMBLE YOURSELF, GET OUT OF YOUR WAY AND APPLY WHAT YOU HAVE LEARNT. IT IS NOT THAT HARD TO GET BETTER AND DO BETTER. ALL IT TAKES IS WISE COUNSEL, A STRONG KNOWLEDGE BASE AND AN EVEN STRONGER OBSESSION OF PRACTICAL APPLICATION.

Tip #123:

Ask your customers who they consider your competitors to be – this can provide some surprising insights into your market position.

Tip #124:

It's not enough to just create what you consider to be an amazing product or service; it must be desirable to enough people to make it worth developing a business around. Not every new idea has to become a new business.

"WE HOLD OURSELVES BACK IN WAYS BOTH BIG AND SMALL, BY LACKING SELF-CONFIDENCE, BY NOT RAISING OUR HANDS, AND BY PULLING BACK WHEN WE SHOULD BE LEANING IN."
– SHERYL SANDBERG, COO OF FACEBOOK

Tip #125:

Get your products into the hands of your customers as swiftly as possible. Shop around and find a courier service that works best for you and your customers. Decide between using royal mail (and look into investing in a franking machine) and other economy couriers such as Yodel, MyHermes and CollectPlus. Stick with one company, look into getting a contract and establish a good working relationship with them.

Tip #126:

If you sell a physical product, be careful with stock. While it might seem more convenient to have plenty of everything to hand, leaving thousands of pounds worth of merchandise on the shelves for long periods of time is a serious cash flow killer. Strike the balance by having enough, getting a good discount on bulk buys, but not burdening yourself with unsold goods.

TIP #127:

IF MANAGING CASH FLOW IS THE MOST
IMPORTANT DAY-TO-DAY BUSINESS SKILL,
CULTIVATING YOUR CUSTOMERS IS THE BEST
LONG-TERM STRATEGY FOR PROVIDING A STABLE
INCOME. MOST CUSTOMERS WILL APPRECIATE
RECEIVING OCCASIONAL INTERESTING &
RELEVANT EMAILS, PERSONAL TOUCHES AND
COMPLIMENTARY GIFTS FROM YOU.

Tip #128:

Look into, and get into video marketing. A clear straight-to-the-point video can go a long way. The biggest advantage of video marketing is that it can be used to generate website traffic from multiple sources. Start working towards creating a 15-30 second video in the form of an ad and aim it towards targeted customers. You don't need no fancy equipment or videography team. An iPhone and a good video app will do. A brilliant 5 second pitch on a 30 second YouTube Ad could result in millions of added revenue and profit. Look into, and get into it.

Tip #129:

A FLYER OR BROCHURE IS MORE LIKELY TO BE NOTICED AND RESPONDED TO IF IT'S HANDED OUT PERSONALLY TO POTENTIAL CUSTOMERS. PREFERABLY WITH A PERSONAL TOUCH. IT MAKES A MASSIVE DIFFERENCE.

TIP #130:

THERE'S NOTHING MORE IMPORTANT TO THE SUCCESS OF AN ONLINE MARKETING CAMPAIGN THAN FINDING THE RIGHT KEYWORDS. THEY DETERMINE WHO WILL FIND YOU. JUST LIKE YOU WOULD IN BUSINESS NETWORKING SCENARIOS, CHOOSE YOUR WORDS WISELY.

"THE THING YOU FEAR MOST HAS NO POWER. YOUR FEAR OF IT IS WHAT HAS THE POWER. FACING THE TRUTH REALLY WILL SET YOU FREE."
– OPRAH WINFREY, AMERICAN MEDIA MOGUL & BILLIONAIRE

TIP #131:

ADWORDS. PAY PER CLICK. GOOGLE ANALYTICS. AD GROUPS. S.E.O. WITHOUT THESE, MAKING MONEY FROM THE INTERNET WILL REMAIN A MYTH AND A MYSTERY.

TIP #132:

BEFORE HIRING NEW STAFF, REMEMBER THAT YOU HAVE TO: PAY AT LEAST THE NATIONAL MINIMUM WAGE AND GIVE A PAY STATEMENT EVERY TIME YOU DO SO, CHECK WHETHER YOUR EMPLOYEE HAS THE RIGHT TO WORK IN YOUR COUNTRY OR NOT, REGISTER WITH THE RELEVANT GOVERNING BODY AS AN EMPLOYER, GET EMPLOYERS' LIABILITY INSURANCE AND PREPARE TO GIVE A WRITTEN STATEMENT OF EMPLOYMENT WITHIN THE FIRST TWO MONTHS OF WORK. IF YOU DO NOT DO THESE THINGS, YOU ARE BREAKING THE LAW. BE CAREFUL.

Tip #133:

Look into covering your business on all fronts. Most companies need public liability and products liability insurance to avoid any mishaps which result in compensation. Take time to learn the ins and outs of your industry. Do not take anything for granted. Don't leave anything to chance.

Tip #134:

Keep track of the time and effort you are investing in your social media marketing efforts by setting specific & measurable targets, such as increasing traffic to your website by, say, 5% a month or generating 200 hits on your blog. You have to be able to measure social media success before you can really achieve it.

Tip #135:

Learn correct dining etiquette of all kinds. Learn about the various styles of dining and the various examples of cultures in every major region of the world. You may have some opportunity to do business in a random place and it's important you know the do's and don't of culture, fine dining & business lunch etiquette. This could make or break your potential business relationship. Take it seriously.

TIP #136:

ALWAYS REMEMBER THAT SERVICE PRICING IS ALWAYS CREATED & BASED ON PERCEIVED VALUE. SUCCESSFUL BUSINESSES MAXIMISE THEIR PROFITS BY MATCHING THEIR PRICING WITH THE VALUE CUSTOMERS PUT ON THEIR PRODUCTS OR SERVICES. THIS IS A MYSTERY YES, BUT WHEN UNDERSTOOD IT CAN BRING UNBELIEVABLE INCREASE.

TIP #137:
NEVER FORGET TO DIVIDE YOUR COSTS INTO
TWO VERY DISTINCT SECTIONS: VARIABLE &
FIXED. KEEP IT THAT WAY...

"ALWAYS LOOK TO THE NEXT LEVEL. KEEP YOUR BRAND IN GOOD HEALTH. BUILD YOUR REPUTATION AS MUCH AS YOU CAN. UNDERSTAND THAT AS AN INDIVIDUAL YOU CANNOT BE PERFECT, BUT AS A TEAM YOU CAN BE. MAKE YOUR WORD EVERYTHING. INTEGRITY AND HONOUR IS KEY."
-FRANÇOIS BENNAHMIAS, CEO AUDEMARS PIGUET

TIP #138:

CALL YOUR CLOSEST RIVALS AND ASK FOR A PRICE QUOTE. IF THEY PERSONALLY KNOW YOU, ASK SOMEONE ELSE TO DO IT FOR YOU. INSIDE INFORMATION BRINGS OUTSIDE PROFITS.

TIP #139:
NEVER SET CRAZY MARK-UP PRICES IN THE HOPE OF BEING COMPETITIVE. ENSURE ALL YOUR COSTS HAVE BEEN REVIEWED, CONSIDERED AND UNDERSTOOD BEFORE APPLYING YOUR MARK-UP. DIFFERENT PRODUCTS APPLY VERY DIFFERENT MARK-UPS.

Tip #140:

Margins indicate the percentage profit a business makes after applying any sort of mark-up. The higher the margin, the more money you can make from it. If you don't know this, then you are lucky to still be in business.

TIP #141:
LOOK FOR CUSTOMER FEEDBACK CONSTANTLY, NEVER FOR COMPLAINTS TO COME LOOKING FOR YOU. BE PRO-ACTIVE AND SET UP NUMEROUS PROCESSES TO COLLECT CONSTRUCTIVE CRITICISM ON A VERY REGULAR BASIS. TESTIMONIALS AND REVIEWS CAN BE PRICELESS IN YOUR GOAL TO GET BETTER.

TIP #142:
AS AN ENTREPRENEUR, ALWAYS BE AWARE OF
YOUR LIMITS AND YOUR RESTRICTIONS. RUN AN
AUDIT ON YOUR INTERNAL AND EXTERNAL
RESOURCES AND GROWTH OPPORTUNITIES.
AVOID OVERTRADING. NEVER TAKE ON MORE
DEMAND THAN YOU CAN POSSIBLY SUPPLY.
KNOW YOUR LIMITS.

Tip #143:
If you can, delegate dedicated account managers to your most profitable clients. This is the best way to ensure they get your company's undivided and most deserved attention.

Tip #144:

Do everything in your power to instil a family culture at your workplace. Forbid any "blame game" antics from your employees. Encourage staff to support each other and work together so that every customer is completely catered to, understood and satisfied. At all costs.

"MANY OF LIFE'S FAILURES
ARE PEOPLE WHO DID NOT
REALISE HOW CLOSE THEY
WERE TO SUCCESS WHEN
THEY GAVE UP."
-THOMAS A. EDISON,
AMERICAN INVENTOR &
BUSINESSMAN

MoneySmart Books for Business

The Lean Startup by Eric Ries

Think And Grow Rich by Napoleon hill

How Successful People Think by John C. Maxwell

Outliers by Malcolm Gladwell

All-Time Essentials For Entrepreneurs by
Jonathan Yates

The 4-hour Work Week by Timothy Ferriss

Great By Choice by Jim Collins

The Richest Man In Babylon by George S. Clason

The Millionaire Mind by Thomas J. Stanley

How They Started: Global Brands: How Good
Ideas Became Great Global Businesses by David
Lester

Small Business, Big Vision by Matthew Toren

Poke The Box by Seth Godin

Start With Why by Simon Sinek

Grinding It Out: The Making Of McDonald's by
Ray Kroc

The Art Of War by Sun Tzu

The Art Of The Start by Guy Kawasaki

Start Something That Matters by Blake Mycoskie

MONEYSMARTS: THE BUSINESS OF BUSINESS

TIP #145:
NOTE THIS DOWN: IT'S EASIER TO LOWER PRICES THAN TO RAISE THEM.

Tip #146:

When furnishing your office, make sure the layout is set up for efficient working. Start with a basic minimum of furniture & equipment. Organise the office to minimise the time wasted moving about. Consider visitors and the feeling they will get when they step foot in your office. What emotion, idea or philosophy do you want to be felt or recognised? Make sure everything important is within easy reach.

Tip #147:

Shop around for a supplier that can help you save money on calls. Consider paying for a freephone number and consider swapping a home phone for a new business line. But make sure you have a very professional voicemail message. There's simply no excuse for having a silly voicemail message. Don't do it to yourself.

TIP #148:

TAKE WHAT YOU DO VERY VERY VERY
SERIOUSLY. NEVER TAKE YOUR TALENT AND GIFT
FOR GRANTED. SUPERENTREPRENEURS NEVER
TAKE THEIR GIFTINGS FOR GRANTED, THEY
MAXIMISE THEM.

Tip #149:

You are legally responsible to file the company's annual accounts and annual return on time. And that means ON TIME. Before registering your new company, get ready for the director responsibilities. The authorities have no mercy when it comes to time.

Tip #150:

Give back to the community. Find ways to get involved with the locals and make a positive contribution. As a local business, you want everyone to know you...especially your local community.

TIP #151:
THE BIGGEST SECRET TO SUCCESSFUL PRODUCT
BUILDING IS WITHIN THE ASKING OF QUESTIONS.
ASK QUESTIONS ABOUT EVERYTHING YOUR
BUSINESS OFFERS. GOOD AND BAD, LITTLE
FEEDBACK AND CRITICISM IS BETTER
THAN NONE AT ALL.

Tip #152:
Never be afraid to sell something you don't need to help pay for something you really do need. Most times in business, it's a game of priorities.

TIP #153:
UNDERSTAND THAT STRESS & UNCERTAINTY
ARE CONSTANT COMPANIONS OF A NEW BUSINESS
OWNER. LEARN TO MANAGE AND RELEASE
STRESS. NEW BUSINESS OWNERS COMMONLY
ENDURE MONTHS OF SPORADIC INCOME. STRESS
ASSOCIATED WITH FINANCIAL UNCERTAINTY CAN
BE EXTREME & CAN AFFECT RELATIONSHIPS WITH
FAMILY AND FRIENDS. YOU WILL NOT HAVE
DEFINED HOURS OR INCOME AND YOUR
RESPONSIBILITIES WILL INCLUDE ANYTHING AND
EVERYTHING THAT NEEDS TO GET DONE. LEARN
HOW TO KEEP BUSINESS AT THE OFFICE.
BUSINESS HAS NO RIGHT TO BRING STRESS,
WORRY OR DISCOMFORT TO ANYONE. LIFE HAS
MORE TO IT THAN JUST MONEY.

"IN BUSINESS, WHAT'S DANGEROUS IS NOT TO EVOLVE."

-JEFF BEZOS, AMERICAN BILLIONAIRE CEO OF

amazon

TIP #154:

UNDERSTAND THE RULES OF INNOVATION: REMEMBER THAT IDEAS COME FROM EVERYWHERE AND ANYWHERE. REMEMBER THAT YOU CARRY THE LICENSE TO PURSUE YOUR OWN DREAMS AND REMEMBER THAT DATA IS APOLITICAL. SHARE AS MUCH PRE-RELEASE INFO AS POSSIBLE AND FOCUS ON USERS, USERS, USERS. INNOVATION IS ABOUT IMPROVING WHAT ALREADY EXISTS. INNOVATION CANNOT TAKE PLACE IF NOTHING IS THERE TO BE ENHANCED, CUSTOMISED OR DEVELOPED.

Tip #155:

A young company is a learning centre. Or at least it should be. Allow for inevitable mistakes and learn from them. A startup's main purpose is to discover a path for itself before it really commits to a particular approach. Nothing worth remembering ever starts off big. Great things take time, so never despise humble beginnings.

Tip #156:

Once you get a new idea, create your prototype immediately. Users and potential consumers want to test what you are working on and they cannot give advice or criticism on what they cannot touch, use or wear. Get designing and get creating.

Tip #157:

A SIMPLE, UNIQUE AND RECOGNISABLE LOGO AND SLOGAN CAN HELP TO BUILD UP YOUR COMPANY IMAGE. BUT THESE ARE NOT HIGH PRIORITIES FOR MOST START-UP BUSINESSES. MAKE IT A PRIORITY. FIND OUT WHAT SIMILAR COMPANIES LOOK LIKE AND FOLLOW THAT TREND. IN THIS CASE, BEING DIFFERENT WILL NOT NECESSARILY HELP YOU, IT WILL JUST ISOLATE YOU. YOUR LOOK AS A BUSINESS IS SUPER IMPORTANT.

Tip #158:
Identify potential health and safety hazards within your organisation. Assessing risks, and taking steps to manage the risks, is the key to successfully managing and maintaining a good level of health and safety. Provide information to volunteers and any employees, and ask them if they are aware of any health and safety risks. Check instructions on any supplies or machinery you purchase and make sure you follow them diligently. This is not an option, it's a legal requirement.

Tip #159:

Take handling personal information very seriously. If you keep any personal information on individuals, you must comply with data protection regulations. For example, you must tell people why you are collecting, holding and using their data, keep the information SECURE, use it fairly and not misuse it. Once again, this is not an option, it's a legal requirement.

Tip #160:

Invest in a quality graphic designer and photographer and become his or her best friend. You will need to. Professional design is critical to the image of your business. Doing things yourself may end up costing you money instead of saving you money. Source out really good professionals and keep them happy. It will pay you to do so.

TIP #161:

REALLY THINK ABOUT WHETHER OR NOT YOU WANT TO REGISTER AS A LIMITED COMPANY OR AS A SOLE TRADER. THERE ARE ADVANTAGES AND DISADVANTAGES WITH BOTH SO DO YOUR RESEARCH AND MAKE THE BEST DECISION FOR YOU, NOT EVERY OTHER BUSINESS OWNER FRIEND YOU HAVE ON YOUR CONTACT LIST. WHICHEVER FORM OF BUSINESS YOU CHOOSE, TAKE PERSONAL RESPONSIBILITY FOR IT FROM DAY ONE. YOU NOW HAVE A BABY. CONGRATULATIONS.

TIP #162:

UNDERSTAND THE IMPORTANT INDUSTRY REGULATIONS IN THE FIELD OF BUSINESS YOU ARE INVOLVED IN. THERE ARE CERTAIN REQUIREMENTS YOU HAVE TO SATISFY BEFORE YOU CAN JUST LAUNCH AND SELL YOUR PRODUCT. IF YOU OWN A FOOD MAKING BUSINESS, YOU NEED TO HAVE YOUR PREMISES AND PROCESSES OFFICIALLY INSPECTED AND VALIDATED BY THE FSA (FOOD STANDARDS AGENCY). BE AWARE OF THE RULES AND STICK TO THEM.

Tip #163:

Never shy away from outsourcing. Infact, if you haven't already...look into it starting from now. Some of your biggest clients will bring business that will force you to look for the best around and outsource. This is one of the best kept secrets in business. Learn to successfully outsource.

Tip #164:

Go premium or mass market. never look for an in-between gulf between the two. It has never, and will never work. Choose one...and dominate it.

Tip #165:
Always remember that businesses are about making PROFIT and that's the Eternal Principle that must inform every business decision you will ever make. Write it on a wall somewhere incase you ever forget.

TIP #166:
TURNOVER IS THE FIGURE THAT REPRESENTS
WHAT COMES IN OVER A CERTAIN PERIOD
OF TIME. PROFIT IS WHAT'S LEFT AFTER
EXPENSES. CASHFLOW IS THE DAY-TO-DAY
FLUCTUATION IN CASH YOU HAVE EVERY SINGLE
DAY. LIVE BY THESE DEFINITIONS AND DON'T
BLUR THE LINES. SUCCESS IS INEVITABLE.

TIP #167:

STUDY THE HUMAN MIND. IF YOU WANT TO FIND BETTER WAYS TO MARKET AND SELL TO YOUR CUSTOMERS, YOU HAVE TO BE A STUDENT OF CONSUMER BEHAVIOUR. TO BE A MASTER TACTICIAN IN THE WORLD OF BUSINESS, YOU NEED TO BE A MASTER PSYCHOLOGIST TOO. THERE ARE ALL KINDS OF TRENDS, PATTERNS & COINCIDENCES THAT YOU NEED TO BE AWARE OF. PAY ATTENTION TO THE WAY THE HUMAN MIND THINKS, INTERACTS AND RESPONDS AND YOU WILL SEE CLUES TO HOW YOU CAN ACHIEVE ACTUAL SUCCESS.

TIP #168:

HAVING MILLIONS OF PROSPECTS ISN'T ENOUGH
IF NO-ONE ULTIMATELY PULLS OUT THEIR
WALLET AND SAYS, "I'LL TAKE ONE". EVERY
SUCCESSFUL BUSINESS ULTIMATELY SELLS WHAT
IT HAS TO OFFER. THE SALES PROCESS BEGINS
WITH A PROSPECT AND ENDS WITH A PAYING
CUSTOMER. NO SALE, NO BUSINESS. AND A SALE
IS NOT ACHIEVED UNTIL THAT FINAL PAYMENT
HAS BEEN MADE. EVERYTHING IS CENTRED
AROUND THE CLOSE. BE A CLOSER.

TIP #169:
EVERY SUCCESSFUL BUSINESS CREATES
SOMETHING OF TRUE MONETARY VALUE.
THE WORLD IS FULL OF OPPORTUNITIES TO
MAKE OTHER PEOPLE LIVES BETTER IN SOME
WAY, AND YOUR JOB AS A BUSINESSPERSON IS TO
IDENTIFY THINGS THAT PEOPLE DON'T HAVE
ENOUGH OF, THEN FIND A WAY TO PROVIDE
THEM IN THE MOST EFFICIENT, CONVENIENT WAY
POSSIBLE. AN ENTREPRENEUR IS A MASTER AT
BEING A SERVANT. IT'S ALL ABOUT SERVICE. IT'S
YOUR JOB TO SORT YOURSELF AND YOUR
BUSINESS OUT SO THAT YOU DO THIS BETTER
THAN ANYONE!

Tip #170:

Restrain from asking "what do you do for a living?" so quickly. Do everything in your power to avoid it. The person you're speaking to is a human first before a fellow businessperson or professional. Work towards gaining rapport and getting to know a person before focusing on the boring stuff. Be cool. Be charming. Be charismatic. Listen more than you speak. Find common ground and make the person like you, regardless of how useful you are to them.

Tip #171:

Organise your calendar, day by day and also week by week. Write down your goals first, clearly state the roles you want to play in achieving them and then follow that up with action plans for each one. There Has To Be An Action To Every Goal.

TIP #172:
DON'T BOTHER YOURSELF WITH AN MBA.
INSTEAD INVEST IN BOOKS, DVDS, CDS, SIGN UP
TO AS MANY BUSINESS-RELATED AFFORDABLE
PROFESSIONAL SHORT COURSES, SEMINARS AND
NETWORKING LUNCHES & DINNERS. SAVE YOUR
MONEY AND LEARN THE FUNDAMENTALS FIRST-
HAND. AN AUTOBIOGRAPHY OF A WORLD
CHANGER CAN GIVE YOU DECADES OF WISDOM
WITHIN 300 PAGES OF TEXT. A SINGLE
CONVERSATION WITH A WISE MAN IS WORTH A
YEAR'S STUDY OF BOOKS. SELF-EDUCATION IS
THE BEST FORM OF EDUCATION.

TIP #173:

TURN EVERY COMMUTE, DRIVE AND EVEN GYM SESSION INTO A POTENTIAL CLASSROOM EXPERIENCE. BUY AUDIOBOOKS AND SUBSCRIBE TO PODCASTS IF YOU WANT TO BE A SERIAL LEARNER ON THE GO. GET INTO THE HABIT OF LISTENING TO SOMETHING EDUCATIONAL, INSPIRATIONAL, POSITIVE AND BENEFICIAL WHENEVER YOU HAVE A CHANCE TO. YOU CAN COVER ANY AREA OF BUSINESS IN A 2 HOUR TRAIN JOURNEY.

TIP #174:
DON'T WASTE TOO MUCH TIME OR ENERGY ON A
BUSINESS PLAN. CREATE THE SKELETON AND
KEEP IT MOVING. A PERFECT BUSINESS PLAN IS
VERY IMPORTANT BUT IT WON'T MAKE YOU ANY
MONEY. GETTING STARTED WILL.

TIP #175:
THE BEST WAY TO OBSERVE WHAT YOU POTENTIAL COMPETITORS ARE DOING IS TO BECOME A CUSTOMER YOURSELF. BUY AS MUCH AS YOU CAN OF WHAT THEY OFFER. OBSERVING YOUR COMPETITION FROM THE INSIDE CAN TEACH AN INCREDIBLE AMOUNT ABOUT THE MARKET: WHAT VALUE THE COMPETITOR PROVIDES, HOW THEY SELL, WHAT THEY CHARGE, HOW THEY MAKE CUSTOMERS HAPPY, AND MOST IMPORTANTLY, WHAT THEY ARE MISSING. GO UNDERCOVER AND STUDY THE COMPETITION. THANKS JOSH.

TIP #176:

NEVER GO INTO BUSINESS FOR THE MONEY ALONE. NEVER EVER. IT WILL ONLY END IN HEARTBREAK. THEY SAY "MONEY IS THE MOTIVATION" BUT IT'S A LIE. FREEDOM IS.

TIP #177:

FIND WAYS TO SCALE YOUR ONLINE BUSINESS AND REDUCE YOUR TIME SACRIFICE. RAISE YOUR RATES IN A WAY THAT INCREASES YOUR REACH. REEL THEM IN WITH SOMETHING AFFORDABLE & VALUABLE AND RAISE YOUR RATES FOR THE BEST CLIENTS WHO ARE WILLING TO PAY TOP DOLLAR FOR WHAT YOU HAVE TO OFFER. THIS IS HOW TO SCALE YOUR ONLINE PRODUCT. THIS IS THE SECRET TO ONLINE BUSINESS SUCCESS.

"FAILURE IS SIMPLY THE OPPORTUNITY TO BEGIN AGAIN, THIS TIME MORE INTELLIGENTLY."
– HENRY FORD, AMERICAN INDUSTRIALIST, FOUNDER OF THE FORD MOTOR COMPANY

Tip #178:
Approach business with the mind of a child. Have an open mind. Kids say what they want to do and actually do it. Be more child-like.

Tip #179:

Understand the full concept of Opportunity Cost. There is always a price, a real all-things-considered price. Nothing is ever free in business (even if no money is exchanged). Test this. Believe this. The best entrepreneurs always know the true cost of every and any transaction that takes place. Become a master at this.

TIP #180:
GET PROTECTED. COPYRIGHTS, PATENTS, TRADEMARKS. DO YOUR HOMEWORK AND MAKE SURE YOU DO WHATEVER IS NECESSARY TO PROTECT WHAT YOU HAVE BUILT. SOMEWHERE SOMEHOW PEOPLE HAVE SIMILAR IDEAS TO YOURS AND IF YOU DO NOT WORK OUT HOW TO TACKLE THE INTELLECTUAL PROPERTY GAME, THINGS COULD GET REALLY MESSY.

Tip #181:

People will pay close to ANYTHING for a specialised niche bespoke product or service. Do not be afraid to pick a price point that isolates you as an expert in your field. For every person that is looking for the cheapest, most common option, there are about three people looking for the VERY BEST. Sometimes it's just a matter of wording. Describe yourself properly for the client you want to attract and you will attract them.

Tip #182:

There's nothing wrong with taking a break or having a 30 minute power nap. Don't rely on high doses of caffeine and sugar for energy boosts. Sleep is the best cure. Taking a break isn't a sign of weakness or laziness...it's a recognition of a fundamental human need: REST.

TIP #183:

TAKE THIS POINT TO THE BANK AND CASH IT:
IT DOES NOT MATTER IF YOU TURN OVER
£100,000 IN REVENUE IF YOU HAVE SPENT
£250,000 TO GET IT. PROFIT IS SANITY,
TURNOVER IS VANITY. FOCUS ON WHAT
MATTERS MOST. THANKS THEO.

TIP #184:
IDEAS ARE CHEAP. WHAT COUNTS IS THE ABILITY TO CONVERT OR TRANSLATE AN IDEA INTO REALITY. SUCCESSFUL BUSINESS IS ALL ABOUT CONVERSIONS AND TRANSLATIONS OF INTANGIBLE THINGS (TIME, ENERGY, KNOWLEDGE, IDEAS, CONNECTIONS, SKILLS) INTO TANGIBLE THINGS (CASH, ASSETS, INVESTMENTS).

Tip #185:

When pitching to investors, follow these rules: Make the exit & reward strategies very clear. Tell a story and make it interesting. Set a clear timeline and deadline. Let them know about all the other people involved. Mention as many numbers as possible and talk big on previous or pending sales. Keep the pitch simple. Reveal a valuation that reflects ambition not naivety. Be BOLD. Be confident. Know your audience, do your research on your potential investors. And SMILE.

Tip #186:

Look into crowdfunding. Crowdfunding is fun, exciting, validating, and relevant. Kickstarter is a great business that can help you raise crazy amounts of cash for even crazier ideas. However, it does cost money so learn & understand the real costs and real reasons to crowd-fund your project.

TIP #187:

GET ON GOOGLE HANGOUTS NOW. IT'S
ONE OF THE BEST OUTLETS FOR BUILDING YOUR
PERSONAL BRAND. GOOGLE HAVE INVESTED
BILLIONS OF DOLLARS INTO THEIR SOCIAL MEDIA
PLATFORMS. IT'S FOR A REASON. AS A BUSINESS
OWNER, YOU WANT TO WHEREVER THE CROWD
IS FLOCKING TO…SO THAT YOU CAN LEAD THEM
TO YOUR PRODUCT. MAKE USE OF IT. BE A
SHEPHERD, SHEPHERDS MAKE GOOD MONEY.

"INNOVATION DISTINGUISHES BETWEEN A LEADER AND A FOLLOWER." – STEVE JOBS, AMERICAN ENTREPRENEUR & CO-FOUNDER OF APPLE

More Tips for The SuperEntrepreneur

Be obsessed with value. Don't be obsessed with products.

Know when to let go. Know when it's time to move on.

Cover all the bases. Be the original not the imitator. But imitate with style & skill if you have to.

The supplier is always at the mercy of the demander. Always.

People buy into the face of a company before they buy from him or her. Be the best face you can be.

Set the stage for growth. Anything that isn't growing isn't living.

Have like-minded conversations and build a bigger more refined network. Build your network before you need it.

Learn to measure everything. Leave nothing to chance.

Always remember: it takes 20 years to build a reputation and five minutes to ruin it. Integrity and character is everything.

The rearview mirror is always clearer than the windshield. Learn to look back and learn.

Network, educate yourself, invest in relationships, spiritually reflect, and take care of your physical and mental health.

Let go of what you cannot control then invest your time and efforts into what you can influence or control.

Decision making is a time-draining vortex. When you're faced with a big decision in the course of your day, give yourself a one-minute limit. 60 secs is all you need to make an instinctively smart decision.

Always, always, always: Stick to your schedule. Always.

Follow the money. In today's economic environment you cannot save your way to millionaire status. The first step is to focus on increasing your income in increments and repeating that.

Prepare to fail. Failure is ok. If you do not fail, you do not learn.

Keep your word. Success is like a house of cards. One foolish act can knock it all down.

MONEYSMARTS: THE BUSINESS OF BUSINESS

TIP #188:

BOOTSTRAPPING IS THE ART OF BUILDING AND OPERATING A BUSINESS WITHOUT ANY OUTSIDE FUNDING WHATSOEVER. SUCCESSFUL BUSINESSES CAN BE RUN WITH JUST PERSONAL CASH, PERSONAL CREDIT, COMPANY REVENUE AND SOME MUCH NEEDED FINANCIAL WISDOM. DON'T BELIEVE THE LIE THAT YOU CANNOT MAKE IT WITHOUT FUNDING. BOOTSTRAP FOR AS LONG AS YOU CAN. IT WILL TAKE YOU FURTHER THAN YOU CAN EVER GO.

Tip #189:
Packaging is a PRODUCT in itself.
It introduces, protects, and displays.
It showcases the story of your brand.
Prioritise packaging and let it tell
your company's story.
Excellence is Everything.

TIP #190:

SOME TAX TIPS: IN THESE CHALLENGING ECONOMIC TIMES, IT MAKES SENSE FOR SMALL BUSINESS OWNERS TO MAKE SURE THAT THEY AREN'T OVERPAYING CORPORATION TAX. AUTOMATIC PENALTIES ARE NOW IMPOSED IF YOU DO NOT FILE YOUR SELF ASSESSMENT TAX RETURN ON TIME. PUT ANY MOBILE PHONE YOU HAVE IN THE BUSINESS NAME AND ALL COSTS OF THE PHONE ARE DEDUCTIBLE (YOU DO NOT HAVE TO SPLIT BUSINESS VS NON-BUSINESS CALLS). TAXATION IS A NECESSARY PART OF ANY BUSINESS, BUT NOBODY WANTS TO PAY MORE THAN THEY HAVE TO. TAKE TAX SERIOUSLY. TIMES ARE TOUGH, SO NOW MORE THAN EVER, WHY PAY MORE TAX THAN YOU HAVE TO?

Tip #191:

Bad employees will eat up your time with constant problems (so best to hire the right ones and train them well). Good employees will waste your time with their well-intentioned attempts to garner your attention (aka teacher's pet syndrome). Love your employees, engage with them when necessary but avoid your employees at all costs. Your job as a small business owner is very different from the job of your employees.

Tip #192:

Get into the habit of completing full days of time logging. Grab a sheet of paper or a spreadsheet (depending on your own preferences) and start from the moment you wake up to the moment you hit the sack at night. Your job is to track every single minute of your day, listing each task and the total amount of time spent. Time is Money, and if you want to make money, you simply need to track everything.

Tip #193:

If a marketing tool is working, stick with it. Too many businesses scrap old promotions and create new ones because they're bored with their current campaign. That's a waste. You shouldn't create new ads or promotions if your existing ones are still accurate and effective. You should run your ads for as long as your customers read and react to them. Don't get emotional. Stick with what works.

Tip #194:

Facebook advertising is one of the greatest ways for personal brands to immediately start building exposure. Creating a Facebook Custom Audience for your personal brand is as simple as visiting the Ads Manager menu then following the instructions step-by-step in what is about a 30 minute process. The next time your business creates an ad campaign you will be able to select a targeted audience of leads already captured who are familiar with what you have to offer, which will help your brand produce more sales. Focus on Custom Audiences.

TIP #195:
SEVEN TYPES OF INSURANCE YOU MAY NEED:
PROFESSIONAL LIABILITY. PROPERTY.
WORKER'S COMPENSATION.
CONTENT. PRODUCT LIABILITY.
BUSINESS INTERRUPTION. CAR.

Tip #196:

Ask potential investors for references, and follow up with entrepreneurs they've backed. Look for investors who contribute additional assets like business development, hiring prowess or executive training. They have to offer more than just their money.

TIP #197:
BE DISCERNING.
SELECTIVITY CREATES SUCCESS. YOU MUST
THINK DEEPLY AND INTELLIGENTLY ABOUT THE
BIGGER PICTURE AND WHAT IT IS YOU NEED FOR
EACH STEP ALONG THE WAY TO CONTINUE
ARTICULATING AND EXECUTING YOUR BUSINESS
GOALS. BE VERY DISCERNING.

TIP #198:

BE WHERE THE BUYERS ARE. FOLLOW THE MONEY. eBAY HAVE 155 MILLION ACTIVE USERS. AMAZON HAVE ABOUT 240. FACEBOOK HAVE 1.3 BILLION USERS. ITUNES HAVE 800 MILLION ACCOUNT HOLDERS. HOW CAN THESE NUMBERS BE OF USE TO YOU? WHEN ADVERTISING AND PROMOTING YOUR PRODUCT OR SERVICE, DON'T JUST GO WHERE PEOPLE ARE, GO WHERE BUYERS ARE. YES, THERE ARE 1.3 BILLION FACEBOOK USERS, BUT ARE THEY ONLINE TO BUY OR CHECK IN WITH FRIENDS? YES, ITUNES HAVE 800 MILLION USERS BUT CAN THEY BUY WHAT YOU HAVE TO OFFER? BE SPECIFIC AND BE WHERE YOUR POTENTIAL BUYERS ARE, NOT JUST WHERE THE BIGGEST CROWDS REGULARLY CONGREGATE.

Tip #199:

Understand the meaning of your chosen name, listen to the way it sounds & carefully choose the name you want to be known by across the whole world. It might not resonate well with the people who really matter: The people who will buy and use your product or service. Don't just think of a name that only your family will love, stay away from personal names. The greatest companies in the world (Apple, Amazon, Facebook, ExxonMobil, Google) don't have anyone's name in it for a reason. Never underestimate the power of a good, simple relevant name when setting up a company.

TIP #200:
MARKETING ISN'T ABOUT CHANGING PEOPLE'S MINDS. YOUR JOB ISN'T TO CONVINCE PEOPLE TO WANT WHAT YOU'RE OFFERING. IT'S TO HELP YOUR PROSPECTS CONVINCE THEMSELVES THAT WHAT YOU'RE OFFERING WILL HELP THEM GET WHAT THEY REALLY WANT. IT'S ALL REVERSE PSYCHOLOGY.

Tip #201:

Stay positive. SuperEntrepreneurs are the most positive happiest people in the world simply because they are making positive contributions that impact billions every day. Your attitude, not your aptitude, will determine your altitude. Success is 90% mental.

The True Definition Of A SuperEntrepreneur

A SuperEntrepreneur is A:
Self-Starter
Possibility Thinker
Thought Leader
Visionary
Pioneer
Job Creator
Value Bringer
Innovation Agent
Catalyst for Change
Believer in High Standards
Reservoir of Wisdom & Financial Intellect
Business Expert
World Changer
Positive-Minded Optimist
Brave & Courageous Individual
Economy Increaser
MoneySmart Genius

What Is MoneySmarts & How Can you Be MoneySmart?

MoneySmarts is a culture. It's an idea. It's about understanding life and money and business and people how they all work together beautifully to shape our world. MoneySmarts is a lifestyle. MoneySmarts is a society of leaders and innovators. It's a thought process for driven, ambitious and successful individuals and families who understand that money is just a tool that can be understood, manipulated and used for great purposes. It's a way of thinking. It's a mindset. It's a belief system. It's knowing that regardless of age, past, mentality, experience (or lack of it), anyone can become wealthy and prosperous. To be MoneySmart is to be wise with your finances, to be MoneySmart is to be literally...smart with your money. To be MoneySmart is to be financially free, financially healthy and financially in charge. It's making the right choices, it's waiting for your turn in life when riches and abundance will flow freely, because of wise and enlightened decisions. To be MoneySmart is to be a money maker. It's being an investor, it's being a creator, generator and incubator of wealth. To be a MoneySmart individual is to be someone who budgets their money wisely, saves their money efficiently, gives away their money generously, invests their money effectively and spends their money freely! If you want to learn more...we have plenty other titles that will help every other important area of your life. Your new MoneySmart life begins right now.

MoneySmarts Business Dictionary
(In case you need it!)

Account - A formal record of the debits and credits relating to the person or business.

Asset - Something that you own that is convertible to cash. Anything that makes you money is an asset.

Bonds - These are certificates sold by companies or governments to raise money. It's a type of investment.

Borrowing - Taking or obtaining something with the promise to return the same or an equivalent.

Brand - A word, name, symbol used by an organisation, manufacturer or merchant to identify its products distinctively.

Break-even - The point in a business venture when profits equal the costs.

Budget - A budget is a calculated estimate of expected income and expense for a given period in the future.

Business Model - The method of which an organisation creates, delivers, and captures value.

CAPITAL – THIS IS ANY FORM OF WEALTH USED OR CAPABLE OF BEING USED IN THE PRODUCTION OF MORE WEALTH.

CEO - MEANS CHIEF EXECUTIVE OFFICER. OFTEN THE OWNER OF A COMPANY. THEY RUN THINGS IN THE BUSINESS AND USUALLY MAKE THE MOST IMPORTANT DECISIONS IN THE COMPANY.

COMMISSION - A SUM OR PERCENTAGE ALLOWED TO AGENTS AND SALES REPRESENTATIVES FOR THEIR SERVICES.

COMPANY CULTURE - THE PERSONALITY OF AN ORGANISATION FROM THE EMPLOYEE PERSPECTIVE; THE COMPANY'S MISSION, EXPECTATIONS AND WORK ATMOSPHERE.

CREDIT - THIS HAS VARIOUS MEANINGS: IT CAN MEAN REPUTATION OF SOLVENCY, ENTITLING A PERSON TO BE TRUSTED IN BUYING OR BORROWING. IT CAN MEAN A SUM OF MONEY DUE TO A PERSON (HE HAS AN OUTSTANDING CREDIT OF £50). IT CAN ALSO MEAN AN ENTRY OF PAYMENT OR VALUE RECEIVED ON AN ACCOUNT.

COST - THE PRICE PAID TO BUY, ACQUIRE, PRODUCE, ACCOMPLISH, OR MAINTAIN ANYTHING.

DEBT - DEBT IS SOMETHING THAT IS OWED OR THAT ONE IS BOUND TO PAY TO OR PERFORM FOR ANOTHER.

DEMAND - A MEASURE OF HOW MANY PEOPLE WANT TO BUY A PARTICULAR GOOD OR SERVICE.

DEPOSIT - ANYTHING GIVEN AS SECURITY OR IN PART PAYMENT.

DIVIDEND - A SUM OF MONEY PAID TO SHAREHOLDERS OF A CORPORATION OUT OF COMPANY EARNINGS. A DIVIDEND IS A PERIODIC CASH PAYMENT (USUALLY QUARTERLY) MADE TO INVESTORS.

DIVERSIFICATION - A MEANS OF MANAGING RISK BY INVESTING IN SEVERAL DIFFERENT INVESTMENT TYPES.

ECONOMY - THE WAY A COUNTRY MANAGES ITS MONEY AND RESOURCES.

EMPLOYEE - A PERSON WORKING FOR ANOTHER PERSON OR A BUSINESS FIRM FOR PAY.

EMPLOYMENT - AN OCCUPATION BY WHICH A PERSON EARNS A LIVING; WORK; JOB; BUSINESS.

ENTREPRENEUR - AN PERSON WHO ORGANISES AND MANAGES A BUSINESS UNDERTAKING, ASSUMING THE RISK FOR THE SAKE OF PROFIT. AN ENTREPRENEUR SEES AN OPPORTUNITY, MAKES A PLAN, STARTS A BUSINESS, MANAGES IT AND RECEIVES THE PROFITS.

EQUITY - THE MONETARY VALUE OF A PROPERTY OR BUSINESS BEYOND ANY AMOUNTS OWED ON IT IN MORTGAGES, CLAIMS, LIENS ETC.

EXPENSE - THE COST OR CHARGE OF SOMETHING. AN EXPENSE CAN ALSO BE SEEN AS A CAUSE OR OCCASION OF SPENDING.

EXIT STRATEGY - A PLAN FOR GETTING OUT OF A DIFFICULT OR UNFAVOURABLE SITUATION. A PLAN THAT MAXIMISES PROFITS WHEN LIQUIDATING INVESTMENTS OR A BUSINESS.

FRANCHISING - THE PRACTISE OF LEASING FOR A PRESCRIBED PERIOD OF TIME THE RIGHT TO USE A FIRM'S SUCCESSFUL BUSINESS MODEL AND BRAND.

FREELANCE WORKER - A PERSON WHO CONTENDS ON A PROJECT OR IN A SUCCESSION OF VARIOUS PROJECTS, OR JOBS, AS HE OR SHE CHOOSES, WITHOUT PERSONAL ATTACHMENT OR ALLEGIANCE.

GIFT - A SPECIAL SKILL, ABILITY OR TALENT; YOUR POTENTIAL SOURCE OF WEALTH.

GOODS - POSSESSIONS, ESPECIALLY MOVABLE EFFECTS OR PERSONAL PROPERTY.

GOOD CREDIT - THE ABILITY TO BORROW MONEY.

GROSS PROFIT - THIS IS THE DIFFERENCE BETWEEN THE PRICE AT WHICH IT'S SOLD, AND THE PER-UNIT COSTS OF LABOR AND MATERIALS TO PRODUCE THAT UNIT. FOR EXAMPLE, IF SOME ELECTRONIC DEVICE COSTS THE FIRM £20 IN LABOR AND MATERIALS, AND IT SELLS FOR £50, THE GROSS PROFIT IS £30 ON EACH UNIT.

INCOME - THE MONETARY PAYMENT RECEIVED FOR GOODS OR SERVICES, OR FROM OTHER SOURCES, SUCH AS RENTS OR INVESTMENTS; MONEY COMING IN.

INSOLVENCY - THE CONDITION OF NOT BEING ABLE TO SATISFY CREDITORS OR DISCHARGE LIABILITIES, EITHER BECAUSE LIABILITIES EXCEED ASSETS OR BECAUSE OF INABILITY TO PAY DEBTS AS THEY MATURE; BANKRUPTCY.

INFLATION - A RISE IN THE GENERAL LEVELS OF PRICES.

INTEREST - THE FEE FOR USING SOMEONE ELSE'S MONEY. IT'S USUALLY CALCULATED AS A PERCENTAGE OR A RATE (SEE INTEREST RATE). INTEREST IS MONEY THE BANK PAYS YOU FOR LETTING YOU TAKE CARE OF YOUR MONEY.

INTEREST RATE - THE PERCENTAGE AT WHICH INTEREST IS CHARGED OR PAID. FOR EXAMPLE, IF YOU BORROW £100 AT AN ANNUAL INTEREST RATE OF 4%. AT THE END OF ONE YEAR, YOU WILL OWE £104 (£100 + £4).

INVENTORY - A COMPLETE LISTING OF MERCHANDISE OR STOCK ON HAND, WORK IN PROGRESS, RAW MATERIALS, FINISHED GOODS ON HAND, ETC., MADE EACH YEAR BY A BUSINESS.

INVESTING - THIS MEANS PUTTING MONEY TO USE, BY PURCHASE OR EXPENDITURE, IN SOMETHING OFFERING POTENTIAL PROFITABLE RETURNS, AS INTEREST, INCOME, OR APPRECIATION IN VALUE.

INVESTMENT - THIS IS ANYTHING THAT IS PURCHASED WITH THE HOPE THAT IT WILL GENERATE INCOME OR BECOME MORE VALUABLE AT A FUTURE DATE.

JOB TURNOVER - THIS IS THE RATE AT WHICH AN EMPLOYER LOSES AND GAINS EMPLOYEES; HOW LONG EMPLOYEES TEND TO STAY.

LEVERAGE - BORROWING TO INVEST. IT'S THE USE OF A SMALL INITIAL INVESTMENT, CREDIT, OR BORROWED FUNDS TO GAIN A VERY HIGH RETURN.

LOAN - MONEY BORROWED FROM THE BANK OR FROM A PERSON.

LIABILITY - This is the opposite of assets. Liabilities include debt, obligations, money owed. Anything that costs you more money than it generates is classed as a liability.

MARKETING - The activities involved in the transfer of goods from the producer or seller to the consumer or buyer come under the concept of marketing. This includes advertising, shipping, storing and selling.

MARKETPLACE - A place where buyers and sellers convene for the sale of goods.

MARKET CAPITALISATION - The size of a corporation measured as the total currency (pound/dollar) value of all of the company's shares outstanding.

MORTGAGE - A loan used to buy a house.

NET PROFIT - The actual product made on a business transaction or sale during a specific period of business activity, after deducting all costs.

MILLENNIAL - A generation born in the late 1980's, 1990's and early 2000's; The best generation in the world today.

MONEYSMART - Being financially wise, regardless of your age or experience; knowing how to handle money, understand money and make money; a state of financial wholeness.

OVERDRAFT - The act of overdrawing a bank account.

OVERDRAWING - THIS IS DRAWING UPON AN ACCOUNT OR ALLOWANCE IN EXCESS OF THE BALANCE STANDING TO ONE'S CREDIT OR AT ONE'S DISPOSAL. THIS IS GOING BEYOND YOUR ACCOUNT'S LIMIT TO TAKE OUT OR USE MONEY BORROWED FROM THE BANK.

OWNER'S DRAW - MONEY TAKEN OUT FROM THE COMPANY'S REVENUE BY THE OWNER FOR PERSONAL USE.

PORTFOLIO - A GROUP OF ASSETS HELD AT ONE TIME.

RECESSION - A DROP IN ECONOMIC GROWTH THAT LASTS AT LEAST SIX MONTHS. IN RECESSION, BUSINESSES STRUGGLE TO SELL GOODS AND SERVICES.

SAVINGS ACCOUNT - A BANK ACCOUNT WHERE MONEY IS KEPT SO THAT IT CAN GROW. WHEN YOU OPEN A SAVINGS ACCOUNT, YOU CAN DEPOSIT MONEY INTO THE ACCOUNT OR WITHDRAW MONEY FROM THE BANK. THIS MONEY EARNS INTEREST FROM THE BANK. THE MORE MONEY YOU PUT IN YOUR SAVINGS ACCOUNT, AND THE LONGER YOU LEAVE IT THERE FOR, THE MORE INTEREST YOU'LL GET.

SHARE - AN EQUAL FRACTIONAL PART INTO WHICH THE CAPITAL STOCK OF A JOINT-STOCK COMPANY OR A CORPORATION IS DIVIDED. YOU CAN OWN VARIOUS COMPANY STOCK AND WITHIN THAT STOCK YOU HAVE INDIVIDUAL SHARES OF A PARTICULAR COMPANY.

START-UP - A COMPANY, PARTNERSHIP OR ORGANISATION DESIGNED TO SEARCH FOR A REPEATABLE AND SCALABLE BUSINESS MODEL.

STOCK - An ownership interest in a company. Stocks are sold by companies to raise money. When a person buys stock in a company, that person owns a tiny part of that company and owns a collection of individual shares.

STOCK MARKET - A place where stocks, or part-ownership in companies, are bought and sold. The New York Stock Exchange (NYSE) is the biggest stock market in America.

TAXES - This is a payment towards the government. There are different kinds of tax (income tax and sales tax). Income tax is where workers pay a sizeable percentage of their income or salary to the government. Sales tax is where people pay a bit extra when they spend in a store.

TURNOVER - The amount of money taken in by a business in a period of time. It's the turning over of the capital or stock of goods involved or the number of times assets are replaced and reinvested over a certain period.

WAGES - Money that is paid or received for work or services, as by the hour, day, or week.

Other Titles by Eric Smarts

MoneySmarts: The Business Edition

MoneySmarts: The Family Edition

MoneySmarts: The Youth Edition

MoneySmarts: The Investing Edition

MoneySmarts: The Kid Edition

MoneySmarts: The Property Edition